Hints of Reality

Reality is Jesus, Jesus is life

Martin H. Perry

Kingdom Publishers

Hints of Reality
Reality is Jesus, Jesus is life
Copyright© Martin H. Perry

All rights reserved. No part of this book may be reproduced in any form by photocopying or any electronic or mechanical means, including information storage or retrieval systems, without permission in writing from both the copyright owner and the publisher of the book. The right of Martin H. Perry to be identified as the author of this work has been asserted by him in accordance with the Copyright, Designs and Patents Act 1988 and any subsequent amendments thereto. A catalogue record for this book is available from the British Library.

All Scripture Quotations have been taken from the New International Version and the King James Version of the Bible.

ISBN: 978-1-911697-06-0

1st Edition by Kingdom Publishers

Kingdom Publishers
London, UK.

You can purchase copies of this book from any leading bookstore or email **contact@kingdompublishers.co.uk**

To Sally with love

To my son **Ian M. Perry** *for the beautiful cover illustration.*

BURNING BUSH

How burnt the bush without the burning?
Like golden leaves that glint and shine
in flowing balls of sun-heat…..
a sign that called to Moses, turning
from bleat of sheep and task on line
of hill where sky and earth meet….

Phenomena!
Oh, how unsure they make us,
confused in mind they take us
to doubt's inquirer.

But holy was the ground, where standing
he looked, bid shoe-less, not too close –
his question hung unanswered….
Instead, there came a calling, handing
a task's demand that he arose,
to sheep be no more tethered….

Angelic word!
No mood that blazed euphoric,
dark weight of faith historic
was felt and heard.

That flame, which turned no leaves to ashes,
came resting in an upper room,
on those of gathered vision....
They'd seen how life divine sparked flashes
in man who scorned the lethal gloom,
roused truth to global mission....

Messiah's aim!
From dark of time, of world, all freeing
so we, and they, arrive at seeing
the constant flame!

TURNED AND WALKED THROUGH THE RAIN

I turned – I walked away – the rain poured down –
increasingly poured down, grey shredded sheet
but curtain blaze of generosity,
poured down into the dry, the starving mouth,
that painful, dark and arid mouth of ground,
once green, that twisted had been into sand.
I and the world recalled those former days
when vines hung rich with jewel darks of grapes,
great oranges were draped like vestments priestly
on tree communities, while seas of wheat
and barley waved and tossed across the valleys,
where men and women sang their songs of joy
that rhythmed with the flashing swirl of scythes –
the harvest was about us all: elsewhere,
with make-shift lines and rods, sat fishermen,
with bait as tempting morsels for what fish
who silver slid and quivered in the stream....
But that was then! Yes, long ago! Then came
the heat, the searing heat, the unabating heat
which changed the world, made blisters of the ground,
but blisters filled with lifelessness and death!
The seeds were planted, covered by grey soil
that suffocated any hope of crops....

No songs of thankfulness, just wailing lips,
thin chafed by fear, and worry, cracked despair.
No fish, no reeds, no pools in riverbed,
no leaves on broken trees that shaded streams,
the vineyard just a remnant of those vines,
now brittle, brown, and barren – sisters sad
to orange orchards, where rare wizened fruit
appeared, small, wrinkled, juiceless – not the worth
of picking: people, weary, in the hotness stood,
and cried – and wondered when the sun would die.

How often I had cried:
"Why has this world now died?
Will you above not hear me?
Do we enough not fear thee?
Why live we this parched world
in heat's destruction curled?
What can we do, or say
to change each burning day?
Bring back our green field wealth –
restore the people's health?"

But answers didn't come – except a sense
of wrong and guilt – an urge we must repent –
must seek out evil that our life ensnared!
Where might we seek? In hearts of people dying,
in limbs of farmers pointless in their digging?
Or might we find it in the armies' armour
that gleamed with pride-filled gloss from cutting sun –

those well-fed troops made eager for a battle?
Or in that palace of the sleek-skinned king
beside the knife-flash eyes of falsehood queen?
Or at those shrines where lies and pomp adored
were spread, upheld by fat and greasy priests?
Oh yes….that's where we found the cause – the dryness
that filled the land, cascading from dry rivers
in all their spirits – king and priest and soldier.
We rose, we challenged – truth with falsehood fought –
they shouted, danced, they cut themselves in frenzy –
no headway forged they in defence: then we….?

"O come, O holy God,
to this sad, barren sod,
reveal your power and might,
expand afresh the sight
of those now blind in lies,
confessions then can rise –
where true, your mercy give
that, free, new ways they live….
but where the darkness stays,
such evil now erase!"

Down came the fire – was falsehood then exposed –
distorted seen those priestly beings – lost,
removed, their power and influence – collapsed
their world of self-authority, for truth
had acted: then the king, in last attempt
at holding power, engaged himself in battle,

arrayed in armour, royal crown of glory….
but came an arrow, found a niche – and killed.
A rebel, moved by chance, in anger rode
to gleaming, gem-filled palace, sought the queen:
he stabbed, her life was ended, outside tossed
as food to drought starved, snarling hungry dogs!
Across the far horizon, clouds appeared,
they spread across the land – advanced a drizzle,
and then some showers, till that curtain fell,
that drape of water, drops, great drops of life –
the ground grew soft, and hope rose proud – I heard
the sound of singing, world it smelt of freshness,
and then I turned – this lone Elijah – turned
and walked away within the rain with joy!

TOWER ACROSS THE VALLEY

Among the fields on half-way plateau,
Church Cottage homely in its shadow,
stands old St. Michael's church and tower
with trees around like sanctum's bower,

where six bells call some Sunday mornings,
in Summer gleams and Winter stormings,
their echoes round the hills resounding
and into hearts and hearths go bounding:

the cows and sheep continue eating,
a tractor down a lane goes beating,
as in the field the cars come parking,
with drivers on the day remarking:

old oak church door is slowly opened
and words of welcome warmly spoken,
in polished box pews people seated
to share the mood down years repeated:

they come to pray and sing their praises
how life and world at depth amazes,
find much in social order shallow,
and human wisdom often callow

that fails when faced with dark diseases,
and cannot deal with what displeases,
the church is seen as ornamental,
and those of faith thought sentimental:

within the church among the meadows,
the faith-full sense eternal shadows
cast by a Being through creation
who births their certain hope's elation:

at end, from pews, down red church carpet,
outside they walk in Nature's garment
transcending time and space around them,
where God-in-Christ has come and found them:

back to their homes, their work, their playing,
for ever in Christ's Spirit staying,
though good and bad is life, his power
remains as sound as Stawley's tower.

MORE TEA, VICAR

It is a pleasant afternoon,
and nice that you should call so soon –
was it six months last came to church?
But I am pleased you thought to search

and ask me why I've not returned –
it isn't that the Lord I've spurned:
on Sundays I don't get the urge –
another piece of Battenburg?

Of course, you're modern: I'm quite old:
I find the modern rather bold,
new tunes now fixed to ancient hymns,
your organist has oddest whims!

And saying "You" when should be "Thou",
then standing when we used to bow –
I find it all to be quite strange
how you have felt to re-arrange

what suited people down the years,
our generation's filled with fears
that God has liking for guitars,
would banish organs to the stars!

Why it has happened I can't see –
one lump or two within your tea?
Oh, none? Need sugar to survive –
old vicar Jones he would have five:

was such a shame, at thirty three,
died he – another cup of tea?
What was I saying? Don't look peeved,
it's for the older ways I've grieved:

those prayers and psalms they sounded grand –
of course, I didn't understand
but seemed to me it didn't matter,
far better than your Jesus chatter:

seems impolite to speak that way
as if the Lord has come to stay
as sort of mate – I just daren't risk it –
would you like another biscuit?

There's danger in the way you do it,
it scares me so, if you but knew it,
how God is not a distant king
I can ignore – to do my thing!

When Sunday dawns, I rise from bed,
to hear your bells inside my head,
but Tesco has far more to see –
your cup is empty – like more tea?

But really I don't like your ways
of frothy happy styles of praise:
there's better sing-songs down the pub
where I enjoy my Sunday grub.

Why do I come? Recall my Bert,
and get some comfort when I hurt,
but you don't give it any more,
it's all so diff'rent past your door…

I sometimes think I shouldn't go,
it spoils my memories to know
the things we liked no more are here
when I to church go once a year.

You'd like more tea inside your cup,
then, Vicar – oh, is something up?
You look as if you want to weep!
Poor vicar Jones he used to sleep!

THE WIND BLOWS OVER IT...

"The wind blows over it,
and it is gone…"
so tolled the preacher
in quiet voice,
a voice emotion-less,
matter-of-fact, no melodrama,
and so the funeral rippled on,
slow slewed the curtain round,
slow slid the tears
from springs of near-one's grief,
accepting but without acceptance.

But why should they accept?
And why emotion numbness in the priest?
Does caring mean omit the feeling?
Has anger no place in the leaving?

"The wind blows over it…"
the Psalmist said,
"and it is gone,"
when, surely, what he should have said
"The wind has blown it over…"
See how the person's gone,
with all their thoughts,
their foibles and achievements'
museum of their history
where people of their world

would stop, admire and walk away,
has fallen to the gale
whose pressure none can stop,
when whistles it round eaves of time,
a crumbling pile of memory
as they are now,
as all will be
when blows that wind,
to blow us over…

Then let the anger grip us –
there's always more to do:
then let the sadness burn us
when all the faces fade…
Don't bid them gone with stoic numbness,
don't toast their fall with malt less whisky,
don't leave emotions home,
or hid in priestly tones!

The wind has blown,
and they are gone –
feel how the fires of pain,
and sadness…
BURN!

THE CHILD OF THEN AND NOW

They tell of a tale at this time of year
when the lanes are dark and the trees stand stark
in the moonlight's stream that is white and pallid,
chill edged with frost:
the story's told from a distant time
of an infant born when the world was wild
but which welcomed to life an unusual child
in some stable bare and a mother's care –
and all seemed lost.

When our tempests rage, and our storm-clouds roar,
and we know our fires, how they burn within,
so our fear turns to terror,
to a cold, cold dread
that the soul shall never leave the dead….
then the story speaks of that child again,
who became a man, who would die in pain
for a world still wild, and still deeply defiled…
a child of humanity
yet bearing divinity,
who would speak of a heaven to the blinded of earth
with their arms outstretched in monotonous search
for the treasures of peace and the jewels of truth,

for the warmings of love and the freedoms of joy –
a child from the God whom many deny
but to whom go the yearnings, each desperate cry,
who now answers in person,
even to death,
with the gift of his life....

Such was the story of times long ago,
yet the tale of each day...
where his life remains vibrant,
and he's welcomed to dwell
in each stable of faith,
in each heart that would love:
for he lives as a Being of merciful power
to heal and to mend,
release and renew
those whose spirit implores for the gift of new birth,
like that of the child who was born God upon earth.

HIS GREATEST DECISION

Like a frost that steals upon the world at night
it came unknown and unexpected, source of fright
since his world would change, control his powers of choice,
bring no sure guarantee his days would each rejoice,
with the thrill of new adventures, deeds of glory,
a growing reputation round a brand new story:
can't ignore it, hangs around like a playful pet
that wants a game with ball, or whines a pleading fret,
asking, growling, won't let go until the walk's
begun, ignore excuses that its master talks…..
"See the rain – how muddy wait the lane and field!"
or "Feel the chill of Winter, how the fire appealed."
"Aren't you tired – I know I am – let's take a rest."
But it's no good….must choose….the future can't be guessed.

Ah – what might people say?
Can't leave! Here you must stay!
Your duty lies this way:
here's sunshine – make your hay!
Your actions might offend,
much ire on you descend:
was life one long pretend?
To leave would mean the end.

And some would judge you cruel
to break convention's rule,
or morals of the school
where wisdom passes fool!

But the choice remained like seasons force their power
to bud the branch or cause autumnal leaves to shower....
pressures on the mind, and conscience churning wild,
kaleidoscope of sweets before a tempted child....
What to do? And how to do it? So deep! So dark!
There's silence to his prayer, though inner feelings hark –
guidance sounds no trumpets, wise men don't appear,
there's just a mighty battle twixt the dream and fear!
What might be the blessing, what success might come –
the strings of indecision play a steady strum!

What can I do, he thought,
what happiness be bought,
what benefits be caught....
such doubts his choices brought.
In peaceful life he's curled,
ambitions tightly furled,
but if this choice unfurled,
what damage to his world?
Perhaps he'd lose, the cost
would mean his safety's lost,
be loneliness his frost
on snowy ocean tossed,

where none would ever know
the choice he made to go,
his life would cease to grow
and him in death would throw.

Deep inside, he knew, somehow he'd always known,
that choice had ever chased him, daily in him grown:
laid he down his hammer, put aside his nails,
decision had been made – new future now prevails:
time to answer yes to his paternal Giver,
so closed the door, and walked to hills and Jordan river.

HOSANNA DUST

Look at the dust, the diamond dust
that gleams in the eastern sky,
dance with the sun to breeze's quick thrust
cast high by them travelling by.

Hark to the dust, cacophony dust
of laughter and shouts of joy,
voices combine as friendship and trust
unite, and then swiftly deploy.

Rising the dust, dark covering dust
of memory within all minds,
past to the present bursts through the crust
as donkey down road slowly winds.

Search in the dust, that wonderful dust
where future stores hopes and dreams:
man on the ass all promises must
contain in his heavenly schemes.

Frenzy of dust, excitement in dust,
each grain an hosanna loud,
wild the emotion building the gust
that blows through the palm waving crowd.

Falling the dust, resettles the dust,
high promises by quiet replaced:
where that great crowd in fervour was trussed,
lone donkey and man can be traced.

ONE EVENING IN GETHSEMANE

Hummed harmonic chant,
between the lisping cedar trees in clustered clumps
bending in the breeze,
drifts slowly up the drooping slope
of bushy garden there.
Her weary head the moon has long since laid upon
a downy cloudy pillow –
thick black darkness,
heavy blanket resting on the atmosphere,
concealing movement:
fading into silence sombre psalm, and whispered soft
"Amen".
Portrayed against the lighter background of the air –
a shapeless shadow
emerging stealthily from out the trees:
a muttered conversation, and the group
of men, about a dozen, stop
at edge of wide expanse of shaded glade:
some sit – some lie –
a few stand still.
Silence seems to bury them beneath its shroud,
as murmurs cease – and motionless their forms
tranquil lingering.
Breeze zephyrs on,
rustling leafy boughs on statued olive trees.
Pause –
a long expressive pause.

"Peter, James, and John."
The Master forward steps: the trio walk behind
further up the grove.
They glide, their gowns upon the ground:
beneath a cypress stand they still.
Voices ripple,
the three disciples on the soft green turf, beneath
protecting branches, take their seat: the Master then
alone,
head in sadness bowed,
with effort staggers on.
His form, beneath invisible and heavy load,
Begins to crumple, agonised,
upon its knees.
His hands in supplication offer up his prayers.
Short instant, moonbeam
shines upon his pallid face.
His eyes, wide, open, staring –
yearning –
seeking –
and sweat upon his brow.
His lips move silently, imploring,
words that in the wind are muttered.
The moon away departs:
darkness falls:
Beside the coarsened bark,
three watchers sleep,
don't see the Master come .
He speaks –
they wake!
Crest-fallen faces gaze upon the ground.
Once more they settle,
their friend retreated into dark.

Once more unveiled, the moon shines down:
the praying figure's nearly
prostrate,
while all his watchers once again
slumber.
Great beads of sweat from off his forehead
drip:
upon the ground,
drip.
The leaves all rustle, passing through the wind:
a final sigh, it seems.
Returns the Master to his friends:
the lunar light's returned behind a cloud:
he whispers quietly to them,
and they all slowly wake:
the Master looks toward Jerusalem.

By the gate,
told to wait,
army stands,
staves in hands,
naked swords,
knotted cords,
torches light
helmets bright,
mighty force
silent pause,
prepare to catch a man of love
who stands alone on hill above.
File so thin
march begin
up the hill,
wind is still\

birds don't sing –
armour ring:
near the men,
watching them
slowly comes a foolish little man
grinning broadly to himself.

Dark shadows from the torches flung,
so gaily yet so crudely, dance
upon the trunks of all the trees.
The Master stands alone:
his friends can hardly now be seen,
so deeply hidden in the shade.
Remaining eight had long since seen
advancing troops: at first their sleepy minds
slow boggled at the sight, then, as they realised –
Fled!
Afraid –
Fled!
The Master's by himself –
Fled!
The soldiers stagger up the slope:
they halt before the unmoving group.
All eyes upon the Master gaze,
as many folk have done –
but then was as he preached.
Silence reigns as forward comes the little man:
nearing to the group, he smiles into those eyes,
loving him with all their deep sincerity.
"Hail, Master!"
Kisses him!
"Hail, Master!"
No sound – the panting world is waiting.

"Hail, Master!"
All Hell hold back its rampant demons.
"Hail, Master!"
The angels cease their glorifying praising.
"Hail, Master!"
Loathsome greeting: worse this world has never known.
"Hail, Master!"
Those words through the captor's brain are flung –
and bedlam breaks.

They seize the Master, pulling to and fro:
his clothes are torn:
his wrists are cut by biting ropes
around them bound – as he looks on,
still loving
all those angered men.
Disciple, frantic now to bravery,
attacks, and cuts off servant's ear.
Then flees!
And Master heals!
Each and every friend has gone:
surrounded by a sea of hateful faces,
alone he stands.
The orders flow, and soldiers, into line,
begin the downward march:
crack the branches underfoot
as on them Master's dragged.
Some priests and scribes shout out
in joy that their sweet dearest friend is caught.
Across the stones he's hauled:
his flesh is torn, and bleeding free –
but no-one cares,
except one solitary figure far behind

who follows secretly:
and Judas, body, soul and mind
in agony tormented.
The shouting mob out through the gate
triumphantly march off.

Then through Gethsemane,
within the leaves,
whispers low the breeze,
"Amen".

SONNETS FOR EASTER

Good Friday
Scorching heat and hateful tree make slowly moving clock's
painful shadow cast its sundial over Calvary
where life breaks to brittle bits of hanging agony,
while on death the victors smile with many laughs and mocks,
glad the day, the deed, are done, restored their threatened hope,
threatened by the quality within that manhood's strength,
opened to the heart by shaft of Truth's deep searching length,
rending them, with fearsome thought, their power could not cope,
so this day their freedom's back is made their joyous claim
now there passes into darkness he who gave the prod
unto servile, docile masses whom they ruled as god,
peaceful now extinguished be his spirit stirring flame:
      yet some say that broken figure twisted bent so odd
      not just rebel to their state – but Son of Man and God.

Easter Eve
O still, how still, set deep within the chilling tomb,
the darkness deeply dark, so thick beyond all sight,
a body stiffly wrapped in graveyard robe of white,
no movement, sound or sense, where life has met its doom,
that fate enfolds its own in timeless clinging grasp
where none can penetrate, or peer with curious eye,
nor aching grief can reach, though deepest be the sigh –

for here lies death itself, full dressed in ugly mask:
beyond the stone, soft tears a lonely face vacate,
and sobs a burning heart, that saw a dreamed-of life
encompassed in that man ere came his final strife,
and present still on cross midst agony and hate.
> But here the rock remains as sombre epitaph
> that death yet reigns as power for life's steep downward graph.

Easter Sunday
Burst forth, O empty heart, in overflowing praise!
Why did you ever doubt since clearly you were told
that mocking enemy, called Death, could never hold
the one your faithful God did promise he would raise.
So, tears, be dried, let chill of dark be warmed and bright,
for past is death, and all its retinue of grief,
no power to hold that Man upon its jagged reef -
he rises free and glorious, full of heaven's light:
stands naked does the cross upon its barren hill
where fallen victors skulk within its darkening shade,
there sigh for yester-week to change their cruel parade,
that resurrection newness might their lost hearts fill…..
> so come now, praise this Man of living power and worth,
> who won that deathly fight, to bring us deathless birth.

BORN TO IMAGINATION

How long ago was it we chased the lawn
with sense of energy in sinews born:
once vision came, we found a world to conquer,:
the years they flowed, said we could wait no longer,
we strode the fields, the streets, through woody thickets,
approached each task, fast bowlers charging wickets,
exhilarated,
life dominated,
our days, our thoughts, engaged with powers impulsive,
and, even in dark times that proved convulsive,
those deep desires remained to drive us on,
like surging spring commands its river gone,
great challenges, fleet moments, life of choices,
contrasts of angels and of sirens' voices,
awhile elated,
or desolated

when sun was shrouded, dark ways dimmed the heart
and undermined our joys, good set apart,
meant struggled we through hapless, trudging days
until a prompt within restored our praise:
these things proclaim our being, not our age,
though race the young, while old they must engage
with wrinkles rippling on the face, the hair
turned grey, when running tempts they will not dare
without complaining,
but still retaining

that fire, that dream, that love, they breathe inside us,
we know them there, kept safe, can't be denied us,
though closer comes that tunnel, black as night,
that all must enter, seeing there no light,
its silence thundering,
each spirit wondering……

• • • •

The slow, slow march beneath the arch of fate,
with curtains widely drawn aside to wait
the words intoned, sees death enthroned in state,
tears caused to flow with fear new found of late
Cold heartless time throughout each age careers
for mini-second or for million years,
expanse or jot,
it matters not
because……...

• • • •

Black nothingness of death begins to thin,
and grey light over dark moves in to win,
our eyes grow sharp in focus
like Springtime early crocus,
to gaze around at grand eternity
of simple glory, vast complexity
of layered universe on universe,
the galaxies' moon-fragments that immerse
and wave-dance in the sea of space and time,
each one a jewel of candlelight sublime,
they gleam as necklace gracing throat divine,
great clusters random laid like beach design,
each grain of sand a diamond of white,
a bright but soft close interchange of light
unending everywhere
of ceaseless depth and flair:

we gaze with all our senses
at all that Life dispenses:

what once we guessed at but can scarce remember,
are here alive, around us in their splendour,
with colours new, unknown, no mind embracing,
all fresh, inspiring, pure, no ills defacing,
the clothes and sight of all creations
and give our beings ceaseless soul sensations,
harmonic sounds of birds and butterflies
with whirring planets' music concert rise
in beauty, soaring chorus ever blending,
always the same with change that's never ending:
yes, all around us changing yet unchanging,
forever still with joyful rearranging,
great mountains, seas, new creatures, trees and bushes
at which we wonder as the Spirit pushes
our conscious beings, ever more embracing
such wonders that on earth we once were chasing,
a distant glimmering,
now clear and shimmering!

Such deep, deep beauty, gone the secret shadows
of lies and whispered plots – all heaven hallows
the Power above, below, through each creation,
who wholly shares its joy-filled exultation:
within the presence of that Power, aware
are we of many peoples gathered there,
eternal ones, created ones, and rescued ones,
were born, who lived, and died beneath the suns
of every planet, every constellation,
who heard "God saves" give Word of their salvation,

eternally the same,
forever Love the same,

who once washed out our blame,
whose peace replaced our shame,
the Power Divine who frees us,
we know him named as Jesus!

PRAYER IS….?

Prayer is not the reciting of prayers,
not construct of builder's word,
not a meeting agenda or list
that's seeking some need absurd.

Prayer is false when demanding to change
the ways of the Mind Divine,
twists his pattern to please a desire,
guides him how to walk our line.

Prayer is me, the way I am,
not image nor repute,
not my words, though fine they sound
with holiness to suit.

Praycr is sap from root to leaf
which cannot help but rise,
to gain the sun for light and warmth
and growing thus supplies.

Prayer is creature underground
in fear of world outside,
dangers there to maim, destroy,
means sorrows sad abide.

Prayer's the wind whose fate must blow,
the waves that cannot cease,
produce of creation's deeds
as fixed with no release.

Prayer is honesty revealed
to Lord's all-knowing sense,
sees beyond the words as used,
so mocked our thin pretence.

Prayer is being what is real
beneath and through what's said,
truth brings life, releases good,
but lies prayed render dead.

Prayer is bonding with what's real
expressed in constant stream
flowing through each moment's breath
of life as is, not dream.

Prayer is not the reciting of prayers
but wanting the Spirit divine,
not to get what my heart may desire,
but rather with him combine.

SEEING THE FACE OF CHRIST

My seeing you
I cannot look away, and then pretend
no more can you be seen....
too close – not close enough – there is no end
as if you've never been:

perhaps a little closing of my eyes,
like clouds before the stars?
But then inside, I know, to my surprise,
you live where nothing bars

your presence, floating through old memories
of people I have known,
of sacred places and their mysteries,
in crowds or when alone....

a great crusade endowed with preacher's fame,
enthusiastic air,
or quiet room where quiet Spirit came,
and sick man gathered care –

a mighty mountain stark and black
that births a blue-ice stream,
or lonely person with a sense of lack
who clings to hope and dream…

So close I see you, sense you being near,
though I would turn away,
and in my turning bring us both a tear
that down our cheeks must stray,

the tear of sorrow, cross of sorrow born
with acid of our shame,
how you, so close, from us by us was torn,
then on you put our blame.

I look at you at times like these, see etched
the deepest kind of pain,
and yet – amazing yet – your eyes show fetched
our means of life again:

that dreadful, saddest look, which shades your face,
still glows with love divine:
it comes to me – oh such eternal grace –
our beings intertwine.

You seeing me
Yes, intertwined are we,
as things are meant to be:
have confidence, pure confidence
which no one can deny,
let nothing thus decry
the person that you are,
to here I've brought you far,
your reference, make reference
when failings in you weep,
and past regrets flow deep,

should others pull you down
with bitter words and frown –
shun diffidence, false diffidence,
each day I give you birth,
a new day rich in worth:
take pride, it is my gift
to cause your spirits lift
when decadence, sin's decadence
of jealousy and rage
would hold you in its cage,
no matter how things be,
your being will be free
with confidence, soul confidence
for intertwined are we,
how things are meant to be.

My seeing others
Yes, you are sap and I the stem,
your face, O Christ, our flower and scent –
but then blows wind – I'm cold, and bent
by breath of others: how in them

can I detect that holy face
once snarls appear, ambition's aim
demands with dark subversive claim
that I must change and join their place?

Like me, they come from same design,
but attitudes so far removed
from what I've learnt, and I have proved:
can it be true they intertwine

in other ways, that I must look
for other traits as evidence,
and with discernment I make sense
so new ideas be brought to book:

fresh understanding will be mine,
a new-born bonding will arise
and matched with Christ before my eyes
so all with him will intertwine.

REQUIEM IN A PANDEMIC

Prologue
Wuhan,
on cold unbeckoning morning:
a man
consumes his breakfast: births a warning,
a cough,
a rather dry, a hacking, cough,
with sweat
across his brow: the mercury
takes off
inside an old thermometer....
The flu?
Or just a cold-like misery?
Or worse?
Life measuring chronometer
slow bells
for 5 plus million world-wide
past death,
and coffins where more millions cried,

It's global,
no land exempt, can't hide from foes,
though mask
hides face when nurse in armour goes:
are jobs
curtailed, arenas, bars are closed:
can't meet

our loved ones, illness else exposed:
each god
is useless, churches, temples barred:
don't kiss,
don't hug, such distant love is hard:
are locked
our doors, confinement to our home:
for lonely,
for stressful hearts, no place to roam!

Meanwhile
comes unseen reeking Virus sliming near
with allies,
skull grinning Death and smirking Fear!

Kyrie
Be merciful to me, a sinner,
have mercy, lord, have mercy,
whichever lord you are:
it matters not – have mercy now
because I fear the consequences
of this disease,
of any failure,
of my mistakes.
No, I would say I'm not a sinner,
just a fun seeking, life enjoying bloke,
but troubles and their fears
disturb the equilibrium
of mind and heart:
no doubt I have upset a few
along the way….
But then have some annoyed or spoilt
the hoped for content of my time.

A kind of tit for tat, a give and take:
that's life diverse, a working out of things:

but, just in case, if necessary,
should low bad feelings,
or ancient prejudice,
possess a power or truth,
if anyone is there and needs it done,
have mercy, lord, have mercy!

Credo
I believe in something,
or nothing, anything,
anything that works for me,
that makes me feel OK:
or, in times of powerlessness,
someone to yell at, blame or curse,
can unleash frustrations –
though no one's proved they're there,
they can take the burdens I cast off,
means I feel better.
Guess I really must believe in me,
and find a kind of helpful bond
with humanity like me.

Do I believe in life?
I'm alive, suppose I do,
more so when sad, denied or threatened.
After my old age and death?
The jury's out on that one,
but if someone offers more to come,
then that's a bonus:
meantime, I will take my chances,
and, just in case, believe whatever.

Intercession
The sun is shining, fine the day,
but I'm indoors and locked away
because some virus wants to stray,
and none can make it go away

Won't someone hear me,
bring safety near me?

It makes me want to scream and shout,
the experts speak but spread just doubt;
I want an open door, go out
and put my life's desires about.

Won't someone hear me,
bring freedom near me?

This virus wants to catch and kill,
but no one's got a healing pill,
and I've a life I must fulfil,
but fear I won't my longings fill.

Won't someone hear me,
no fear be near me?

It's sad when hearing people die,
bad on TV see people cry,
those deaths and sorrows can't deny,
but my own spirit has to fly!

Won't someone hear me,
and come to cheer me?

I call upon the government,
make sure I get my life's intent,
for cage and death should not be sent,
have years to live which must be spent.

Won't someone hear me,
stop virus near me?

Want life that's realistic,
be not some morgue statistic.

Sanctus
Outside,
the day's permitted exercise,
quiet,
no constant noise and main road traffic:
fresh air,
bird song, stream's ripples, breeze bent bushes,
expanse
of sky ethereal with clouds,
the world
before the virus of pollution,
when rose
from depths eternally constructed.

Behind
pandemic spewing death and sorrow,
closed doors,
each house a little world of self –
out here,
a height, a breadth that's everlasting,
that speaks

of all things living, much forgotten,
vast place
beyond each human's limitations,
beyond
the empty box of science knowledge,
beyond
confines of birth and death's departure,
beyond
our narrow consciousness and wants,
to where
breathes life unending, all things holy!

Agnus Dei
If out beyond you're there as source of life,
though media speak of death and gloom,
please have a thought for me.

If you of beauty, health and comfort are,
though human experts claim the role,
please have a thought for me.

When in the night I fear both loss and death,
and feel are my defences down,
please spare some peace for me.

Though ignorant am I of all things you,
invisible in air and man,
please bear my lack in mind.

If purity and sacred good are you,
to which I gave no thought or time,
please set aside my ways.

When death will come, as come it will, with dread,
I pale to meet my consequence,
please spare some peace for me.

Communion
My narrow confines in vast expanse,
thoughts limited now becoming stretched
by vision, sense, and a mode of thanks,
as if to me there are being fetched

ideas and longings that I had banned,
dead history in my life unwanted,
but now I look and there's something grand
which would engage, as a power undaunted,

my spirit,
which must awaken feeling,
then rearrange the contents of my mind,
inherit
new sense of life appealing
beyond what's known, awaiting me to find.

I reach beyond the world I see,
on hold I put the life I know –
there breathes outside of time and space
vast patient Being calling me,
who would, to heart uncertain, show
eternal vision, power and grace.

I can't explain, but I can feel
a pulsing presence all around,

beyond all things, yet in all things!
What else to do? My life must kneel:
in words unspoken comes their sound
as if a choir eternal sings:

"Here is my body given here to you.
Here is my life blood I pour out for you."

This awesome Power I dare not leave.
It's always here and I receive.

Gloria
The virus roams: we're locked in homes,
but once outside no more applied
are numb edged fears and social meanness,
just blue-bright air and birth-spring cleanness:
cast off the fears with new ideas,
your chains uncurled, discover world –
so much ignored by knowledge, oddly –
which tells of power and values godly:

eternal gifts the spirit lifts
where heart's alive, more than survive,
see through great Nature's fabrication,
detect there high Divine creation –
soft butterflies, pale moon on rise,
sky star-lit worth, new baby's birth –
our Saviour-Word leads his procession
throughout Creator's self-expression:

when this we know, our fears they go,
come peace and joy, we praise deploy,
so hallelujah joins hosanna,
extolling all in every manner:
here is our story, divine its glory,
to our relief, our sure belief,
know all we have and are, our living,
is nothing less than God's own giving!!

www.ingramcontent.com/pod-product-compliance
Lightning Source LLC
Chambersburg PA
CBHW071545080526
44588CB00011B/1804